ALTERNATOR
BOOKS™

MISSION
JAVASCRIPT

SHEELA
PREUITT

Lerner Publications ◆ Minneapolis

TO MY DAD, V.V.S., FOR HIS STEADFAST
LOVE AND SUPPORT

Lerner Publications Company
An imprint of Lerner Publishing Group, Inc.
241 First Avenue North
Minneapolis, MN 55401 USA

For reading levels and more information, look up this title at
www.lernerbooks.com.

Main body text set in Aptifer Slab LT Pro.
Typeface provided by Linotype.

Library of Congress Cataloging-in-Publication Data

Names: Preuitt, Sheela, author.
Title: Mission JavaScript / Sheela Preuitt.
Description: Minneapolis, MN : Lerner Publishing Group, Inc., [2020] |
    Series: Mission. Code (Alternator Books) | Includes bibliographical
    references and index. | Audience: Ages 8–12. | Audience: Grades 4 to 6.
Identifiers: LCCN 2018054256 (print) | LCCN 2018055018 (ebook) |
    ISBN 9781541556386 (eb pdf) | ISBN 9781541555907 (lb : alk. paper) |
    ISBN 9781541573741 (pb : alk. paper)
Subjects: LCSH: JavaScript (Computer program language)—Juvenile
    literature.
Classification: LCC QA76.73.J39 (ebook) | LCC QA76.73.J39 P74 2020
    (print) | DDC 005.2/762—dc23

LC record available at https://lccn.loc.gov/2018054256

Manufactured in the United States of America
1-46046-43462-4/23/2019

CONTENTS

To download files for the Your Mission: Code It! activities, visit http://qrs.lernerbooks.com/JS. You'll need to use the Google Chrome web browser to complete the Your Mission: Code It! activities that appear throughout this book. To download the Google Chrome browser, visit https://www.google.com/chrome/. Always check with an adult before downloading files from the internet.

LANGUAGE BEHIND THE SCREEN

Want to write video games or even control robots? JavaScript is a great **programming language** to learn to do that.

JavaScript is used everywhere! Popular websites such as Facebook, Twitter, Amazon, and YouTube use JavaScript to make their websites fun and interactive. Animations, sounds, and maps with location markers are some examples of JavaScript in action.

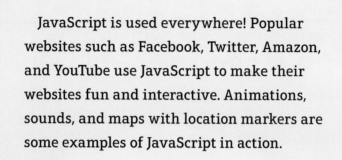

The coders who created some of your favorite websites used JavaScript to make them.

CHAPTER 1
WHAT IS
JAVASCRIPT?

COMPUTERS, BY THEMSELVES, ARE NOT SMART. They can do only what we humans tell them to do. We talk to them through computer **programs**, which are step-by-step instructions written in a specific programming language. JavaScript is one such programming language.

What makes up a programming language? Like other types of languages, programming languages have a specific **syntax**. The syntax includes special **keywords** as well as punctuation. Punctuation could include semicolons, colons, and periods, as well as parentheses and brackets.

All keywords and punctuation in a programming language must appear in a particular order. That's what the word *syntax* means. If something is out of order, the computer won't be able to read the language. It won't do what you want it to do.

Practice makes perfect. Do a lot of coding, and you'll be able to read and write it like a pro.

JavaScript works together with two other programming languages, HTML and CSS, to create awesome websites. It can be used to find, organize, and change pieces of information, or data, that you give to a website, such as when you create an account or log in. It does all of this in the background, so that you don't have to refresh the web page to see all the changes.

There may be a lot going on behind the scenes in JavaScript, but with just a little effort, anyone can learn it. And once you do, you too may be creating an animation or even designing the next best-selling video game!

Anyone at any age can learn to code.

CHAPTER 2

ALL ABOUT THE DATA

ONE OF THE POWERS OF PROGRAMMING LANGUAGES IS THAT THEY CAN MANIPULATE DATA. Data is any piece of information stored in a computer. Your dog's name, your eye color, your age, how many siblings you have, and whether you liked a book or not are all examples of data.

JavaScript uses three basic types of data: numbers, **strings**, and Booleans.

Data such as your age and how many siblings you have are expressed as numbers. In JavaScript, numbers are typed just as you'd normally write them, including decimals. You can even use JavaScript as a calculator. It can do both basic and more complicated calculations.

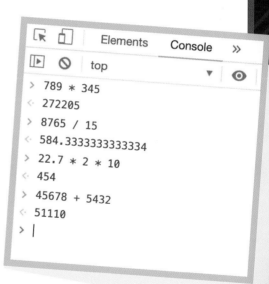

```
> 789 * 345
< 272205
> 8765 / 15
< 584.3333333333334
> 22.7 * 2 * 10
< 454
> 45678 + 5432
< 51110
> |
```

Input lines in JavaScript begin with the > symbol. The output lines begin with the < symbol.

Data such as your dog's name and your eye color are represented by strings in JavaScript. Strings are sequences of letters, numbers, and punctuation. Strings have to be enclosed in quotation marks, like this: "I am a string."

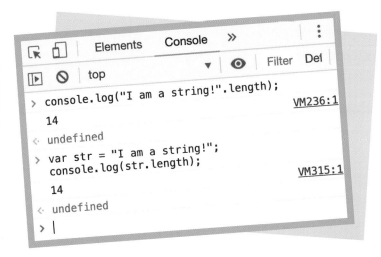

The command *.length* tells you how many characters are in a string.

Finally, data that can be only one of two possible values, true or false, is called a Boolean. A Boolean could be whether you liked a book or not.

Each data type has its own set of possible operations, or ways of working with them. You can multiply two numbers, but you cannot multiply two strings. You can find the length, or number of characters, of a string. With Booleans, you can check if two values are both true. As you work with each data type, you will learn which operators can be used with each of them.

You can turn anything into a piece of data, from whether you liked a book to how many pages you read to the names of your favorite characters.

A **variable** holds a piece of data that you want to use later. When data is stored in a variable, it is called a value. Each variable can have a unique name and hold exactly one value. To create a variable, use the keyword *var*.

```
var myDogsName = "Rover";
var myEyeColor = "brown";
var myAge = 11;
var isBookGood = true;
```

It helps to choose variable names that are meaningful and self-explanatory so that your code is easy to read. Variable names cannot have spaces and cannot be keywords.

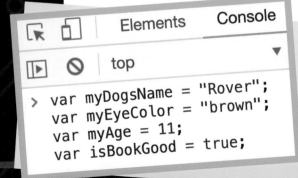

```
Elements      Console

top                        ▼

> var myDogsName = "Rover";
  var myEyeColor = "brown";
  var myAge = 11;
  var isBookGood = true;
```

Many JavaScript consoles use different colors to help show each part of the code. This is how the code might look on your screen.

In the examples on the previous page, *var myDogsName* tells JavaScript that *myDogsName* is a variable. The = sign is the way you tell JavaScript that *myDogsName* should hold the value Rover. Notice that "Rover" is enclosed in quotes to show that it is a string.

Similarly, *myAge* is the name of the variable that holds the numeric value 11. And *isBookGood* holds the Boolean value true.

If your family has a pet, its name could be a variable when you work with JavaScript.

You can change the value of a variable that you have created. When you do this, the keyword *var* is not needed because you are not creating the variable for the first time. For example,

```
myDogsName = "Fido";
myEyeColor = "green";
```

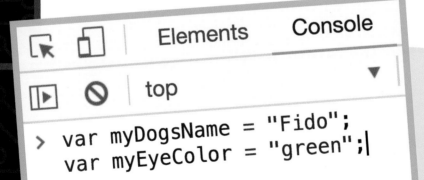

YOUR MISSION: CODE IT!

It's time to try a fun activity! First, open your JavaScript console. Open the Chrome web browser and type about:blank on the address bar. You should see a blank white page. Then hold down the Ctrl and Shift keys on the keyboard and press J. (On a Mac, hold down the Command and Option keys and press J.) A window should appear on your screen. This window is the console. It is where you will type your JavaScript.

Create a new variable named *myFavoriteFruit* and assign it the value "Strawberry." Then type *console.log(myFavoriteFruit)* and press Enter. What do you see? Now, change the value of this variable by assigning it a new value: *your* favorite fruit. Again, use *console.log(myFavoriteFruit)*. What do you see now?

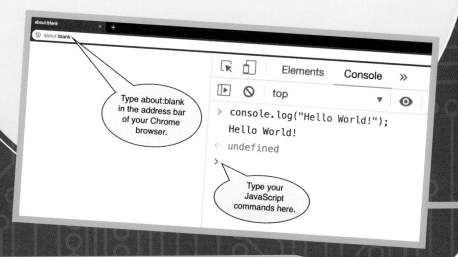

Type about:blank in the address bar of your Chrome browser.

```
> console.log("Hello World!");
  Hello World!
< undefined
>
```

Type your JavaScript commands here.

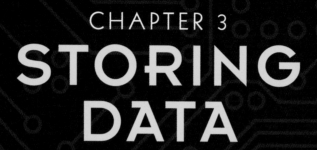

CHAPTER 3
STORING
DATA

SOMETIMES WEBSITES NEED TO
CHECK CERTAIN THINGS ABOUT
THEIR USERS, SUCH AS THEIR AGE
OR LOCATION, TO MAKE SURE
EVERYTHING WORKS CORRECTLY.

Such checks can be done using
comparison operators. Comparison
operators result in either *true* or *false*.

One comparison operator is ===. This operator checks to see if the value and the type of the value of two variables are both the same. For example, while the number 12 and the string "12" have the same value, they do not have the same type of value because one is a number and one is a string.

```
var numericValue = 12; //number
var stringValue = "12"; //string
numericValue == stringValue //true
numericValue === stringValue //false
//The number 12 is not equal to the
string "12"
```

As humans do in real life, computers often need to compare two things to see if they are the same.

There are lots of common comparison operators. Let's create a variable var x = 10 for the examples below. Here, the letter x represents the number 10.

Operator	Operation	Example	Result
==	Equal to	x == 11	false
!=	Not equal to	x != 11	true
>	Greater than	x > 12	false
<	Less than	x < 12	true
>=	Greater than or equal to	x >= 10	true
<=	Less than or equal to	x <= 10	true

Arrays are also important in JavaScript. Let's say you are writing your birthday wish list. You write your first item, or variable, on one sheet of paper. You write your second item (variable) on another. You keep going this way until each item is written down.

```
var myWishList = ["bicycle", "bike helmet", "bike bell", "bike
mudguard", "bike basket"];
```

But you don't want to keep track of lots of sheets of
paper with your wish list items. You want to make
one big list with all the variables written on one
sheet. That's where arrays come in handy. Arrays are
used to represent a list of various things.

Instead of having five different variables in a list
like the one below . . .

```
var myFirstItem = "bicycle";
var mySecondItem = "bike helmet";
var myThirdItem = "bike bell";
var myFourthItem = "bike mudguard";
var myFifthItem = "bike basket";
```

. . . JavaScript lets you create an array with many
items using square brackets.

```
var myWishList = ["bicycle",
"bike helmet", "bike bell", "bike
mudguard", "bike basket"];
```

```
console.log(myWishList[3]); // bike mudguard
console.log(myWishList[4]); // bike basket
```

JavaScript will remember the order of the items in an array. This order is called the **index**. If you ever forget what the first item in your array is, for example, you can ask JavaScript. However, the index is a little tricky, because the first item is labeled with 0, not 1. In this example, "bicycle" is item number 0, "bike helmet" is number 1, and so on.

Here is an example of how to find a specific item in an array with the index:

```
console.log(myWishList[3]);
bike mudguard
console.log(myWishList[4]);
bike basket
```

Let's say you want to store information about your cat, such as its nickname, age, color, breed, favorite toy, and favorite food. You also want to store the same information about your friend's cat and your cousin's cat. That is a lot of variables to keep track of. To help you keep track of all this information, you can create an **object**.

An object is another way to store data. Instead of using an index to access data, as an array does, an object uses strings called keys. Each key is matched to a value. There are six key-value pairs in our cat object—one for each piece of information.

```
var myCat = {
    "nickname": "Fluffy",
    "age":    2,
    "color": "white",
    "breed": "Persian",
    "toy": "paper ball",
    "food": "yummy yums"
};
```

JavaScript can do almost anything you want it to, including storing information about your cat's color, breed, favorite toy, and more!

An object can also be made up of arrays. Instead of a single value, a key can refer to an array. See the example below:

```
var iceCreamsILike = ["rocky
road", "chocolate"];
var myFavoriteThings = {
      "authors": ["Judy Blume", "J.
      K. Rowling", "Walter Dean
      Myers"],
      "iceCream": iceCreamsILike,
      "petsIHave": ["cat",
      "hamster", "goldfish",
      "tarantula"],
};
```

```
var iceCreamsILike = ["rocky road", "chocolate"];
var myFavoriteThings = {
    "authors": ["Judy Blume", "J. K. Rowling", "Walter Dean Myers"],
    "iceCream": iceCreamsILike,
    "petsIHave": ["cat", "hamster", "goldfish", "tarantula"],
};
```

1. Open up the JavaScript console in Chrome again. Create an array called *myTopFiveBooks* made up of your top five favorite book titles.

2. Create an array called *myTopFiveGames* made up of your top five favorite board games.

3. Create an array called *myTopFiveSnacks* made up of your top five favorite snack foods.

4. Finally, create an object called *topFiveThings* made up of the three arrays you created in steps 1–3.

5. Use *console.log* on your object *topFiveThings*. What do you see?

CHAPTER 4

CONDITIONAL STATEMENTS AND FUNCTIONS

EVERY DAY, YOU MAKE DECISIONS BASED ON CERTAIN CONDITIONS BEING TRUE. Such decision-making can be expressed in programming through **conditional statements**. The simplest conditional statement is *if*: if something is true, then do this.

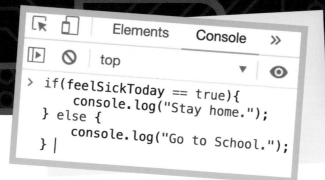

```
> if(feelSickToday == true){
    console.log("Stay home.");
  } else {
    console.log("Go to School.");
  } |
```

What if you wanted to do one thing when the condition is true but another thing when the condition is false? In that case, you can use *if . . . else*. For example, if you feel sick today, you stay home, or else you go to school.

```
var feelsSick = false;
if (feelsSick == true) {
   console.log("Stay home.");
} else {
   console.log("Go to school.");
}
```

When you want to perform the same task over and over, you can write a function. A function is a set of instructions that you give a name. The function acts like a shortcut. Whenever you put the function in your code, JavaScript knows to run all the instructions without your having to write them out each time.

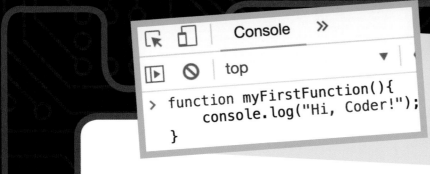

```
> function myFirstFunction(){
      console.log("Hi, Coder!");
  }
```

A function is written as follows:

```
function myFirstFunction(){
      console.log("Hi, Coder!");
}
```

Use the name *myFirstFunction()* to instruct the computer to display the words, "Hi, Coder!"

```
myFirstFunction(); // Hi, Coder!
```

The parentheses next to the function name can contain **arguments**. Arguments can be numbers, strings, Booleans, or even variables. For example, if you wrote a function that checks if a number is even, you can test different numbers as arguments.

Now you have some of the basics of JavaScript down pat. Keep honing your skills. Who knows? Someday you might develop the next great JavaScript creation!

YOUR MISSION:
CODE IT!

1. Open the console in Chrome.

2. Define a function *guessTheNumber* that receives a number, *myGuessNumber*, as its only argument.

3. In the function, create a variable *myRandomNumber* and assign it a number between 1 and 10.

4. Use the conditional *if . . . else* to check if *myGuessNumber* equals *myRandomNumber*. If it does, the function should show, "You guessed it!" Otherwise (else), it should show, "Nope, try again . . ."

5. See if your friends can guess the number!

```
  Elements   Console   Sources   Network   Performance   Memory   »
  top                      ▼  ⊙   Filter                Default levels ▼
> function checkIfEvenNumber(number){
      var answer;
      if(number % 2 == 0){
          answer = number + " is an even number!";
      } else {
          answer = number + " is NOT an even number!";
      }
      return answer;
  }
  checkIfEvenNumber(23);
< "23 is NOT an even number!"
> checkIfEvenNumber(56);
< "56 is an even number!"
> checkIfEvenNumber(789);
< "789 is NOT an even number!"
> checkIfEvenNumber(1752);
< "1752 is an even number!"
> |
```

Use this code as an example to help with the Your Mission: Code It! activity on this next page.

GLOSSARY

arguments: the values given to functions so they can do their tasks

arrays: variables that store lists of items

conditional statements: lines of code that tell the computer to perform different tasks based on whether a condition is true or false

index: the numeric order of items in an array

keywords: words in a programming language that can be used only in a certain way

object: a collection of keys that describe something

programming language: a set of rules that tell computers how to understand programs

programs: specific sets of ordered commands for a computer to perform

strings: sequences of letters, numbers, and symbols that are enclosed in quotation marks

syntax: the rules that specify the symbols, keywords, and allowed words for writing programs

variable: a container for storing data

FURTHER INFORMATION

Introduction to JavaScript
https://www.codecademy.com/learn
/introduction-to-javascript

JavaScript Tutorial
https://www.w3schools.com/js/

Learn JavaScript
https://www.learn-js.org

Morgan, Nick. *JavaScript for Kids: A Playful Introduction to Programming.* San Francisco: No Starch, 2015.

Preuitt, Sheela. *Mission HTML.* Minneapolis: Lerner Publications, 2020.

Young Rewired State. *Get Coding! Learn HTML, CSS, and JavaScript and Build a Website, App, and Game.* Somerville, MA: Candlewick, 2017.

INDEX

PHOTO ACKNOWLEDGMENTS

Image credits: Various screenshots by Sheela Preuit.
Additional images: Caiaimage/Robert Daly/Getty Images,
p. 5; Tuan Tran/Getty Images, p. 7; matejmo/Getty
Images, p. 8; vgajic/Getty Images, p. 9; Hero Images/Getty
Images, p. 13; Phil McDonald/Shutterstock.com, p. 15;
Kasabutskaya/Shutterstock.com, p. 19; rukawajung
/Shutterstock.com, p. 23. Cover and interior design
elements: HuHu/Shutterstock.com (runner); Vankad
/Shutterstock.com (circuits); Bro Studio/Shutterstock.com
(circular pattern); Leremy/Shutterstock.com (figures).